The promised folly

The promised folly

Judith Hall

TriQuarterly Books
Northwestern University Press
Evanston, Illinois

TriQuarterly Books
Northwestern University Press
Evanston, Illinois 60208-4210

Printed in the United States of America

10 9 8 7 6 5 4 3 2 1

ISBN 0-8101-5136-7 (cloth)
ISBN 0-8101-5137-5 (paper)

LIBRARY OF CONGRESS CATALOGING-IN-PUBLICATION DATA

Hall, Judith, 1951–
    The promised folly / Judith Hall.
        p. cm.
    ISBN 0-8101-5136-7 (cloth) — ISBN 0-8101-5137-5 (pbk.)
    I. Title.
PS3558.A3695 P76 2002
811'.54—dc21

                                                    2002014759

Come, let us goe, while we are in our prime;
And take the harmless follie of the time.
　　　　We shall grow old apace, and die
　　　　Before we know our liberty.
　　　　Our life is short; and our dayes run
　　　　As fast away as do's the Sunne:
And as a vapour, or a drop of raine
Once lost, can ne'r be found againe:
　　　　So when or you or I are made
　　　　A fable, song, or fleeting shade;
　　　　All love, all liking, all delight
　　　　Lies drown'd with us in endlesse night.
Then while time serves, and we are but decaying;
Come, my Corinna, come, let's goe a Maying.

—Robert Herrick

contents

the promised
folly

***

The Princess

In taking a state the conqueror must arrange to commit all his cruelties at once, so as not to have to recur to them every day, and so as to be able, by not making fresh changes, to reassure people and win them over by benefiting them. Whoever acts otherwise, either through timidity or bad counsel, is always obliged to stand with knife in hand, and can never depend on his subjects, because they, owing to continually fresh injuries, are unable to depend upon him. For injuries should be done all together, so that being less tasted, they will give less offense.

—Niccolò Machiavelli

Some may wonder how I came to this
And how my violence was meant to "fetter" theirs.
Was that the obfuscating verb?
My violence was meant to fetter theirs,
Not inspire it. Worse theories abound,
And every one of them, my allies urged.

Advisers gathered at my country place,
Rejecting "undeclared wars." But mine,
They were mine! As were the greens and breads
And breasts of albino capons. One last Madeira.

Some manipulations civilize,
Though when I hear now of injuries
They advocate to others for the other side,
Damages "clustered" seductively,
They are, I know, mere souvenir behaviors,
What they took from my maneuverings.

Remember the moon that night? So useful
On the lines of men wandering slowly through
The gardens near the aromatic trees.
On benches there, they caucused for "fraudulence"

Always, the flatulence of celebration.
"Say we won," they shouted at the moon.
And shouting after me, angrily,
"Say we won. Bring the boys home now,"
As if the tired economy bequeathed to me
Thrived on greens and breads and celebration.

It was safer to be feared than loved,
"Much safer to be feared," I learned,
Rejecting their parade, fraud-victory,
Their argument that people loved parades.

Do people love parades? More gray confetti,
The ludicrous nostalgic piccolos,
The fezzed veterans' arthritic flickers:
"Welcome home, my John, my son, welcome
Malcolm, Luke, my Paul, we love you, welcome
Home, we love you, Homer. We won the war."

The other side's parade spills across my land.
I stand "with knife in hand," as he predicted.
What an education in timidity,
And now confetti blows this far, and song.

Fold Here: For United States: Found Poems

: Emerson—Don't tell me: Real life consists of bluffing: They made us:
: To get ready to die. I know: Of little tactics, of deception, of: Many promises:

: Not: Asking yourself: More than I can remember:
: What shall be.: What is the other man going to think: But:

: The only preparation I: I mean: They:
: Can make is: To do.: Never kept:

: By: A theory: But:
: Fulfilling my present duties. This: : One; they promised:

: Is: : To take our land.:
: The everlasting life.: Of games: And they took it.—Red Cloud:

Rumors Play on Rumors of a Plague

Happy are they who have been able to discover the causes of things.

—Virgil

I

Research   once begun   became rumors in the States
When funding floated overseas
For air-conditioned labs
Locked cabinets   Computers flew across the Chesapeake
Metal desks came in and chairs
With Venezuelan leather
It was thoroughly reviewed by upper echelons
To calculate   extrapolate

Manipulate   leaks
Why were we over there   Why anywhere
Someone said   leaning over
To diffuse analysis
Sad   *No one used to ask what happened over there*
What viruses did we inject

In mice   whatever
Before the boy crated them and ran down the back steps

Down the hill to the waiting truck
And when it drove away
He reported animals leaping in the long-dry unmacheted fields
Before they hunted down and raided
The dying specimens
Different rumors on all this circulated   worse
When we were stationed on the hill
Denials varied   but

It cost us more to deny appropriations   rumors on
Our vital interest *in viruses*
Than deny the viruses
And if the spill   and if one man had never   Was he the one
Who ate the brains of animals
Sacred animals

II

Why locals spoke of animals   we funded next fiscal year
And who could verify when   if we

If evidence deleted
Reported as the grousing of a reassigned clerk
That never happened   Senator
When they came to us
With lies on the poisoned yellow field   *yes   reported* poisoned
Inquiries erupted   re
Dumped specimens
The spill   the smell excited carnivores   novelties

Species we prematurely released
Genetic engineering
Sir   is not within the well-nigh distended scope of this hearing
Let me remind you   Senator
As a point of fact
Our work rode in on your bill granting medical Viagra

To officers above a rank
Of colonel   lieutenant colonel

Or by now assuming they too miss their marks   major
Is sex rank's prerogative
With all due respect
Was no pharmaceutical incentive offered to our boys
Noncombatant   overseas
More than caffeinated
Cigarettes manufactured in your Tarheel hometown
Well-nigh contempt   sir   contempt

Then he let his lawyer
Return to rumors like the one new truck backing up was ours
And weather   prophylactic rain
A little in-house joke
On runoff   His geologists testified
To the ratio of slope

To percolation   then
Factoring in viscosity of viruses this hastily contrived

When a postdoc saw the locals
Offer combs for rain
Cigarettes   marigolds   myriad prayers   gourds
Shook with pebbles   shook to change
That was how we met him
Through young lab assistants   boys who knew the language
Dead culture   a culture of death
As you put it here

The burned sugar smell of the nearly dead covers the fields
What is that word   sir   Men
Men poured out like heat
On the field   with nothing to warm and nothing to grow against
When asked to volunteer   this one
Who led the rest in prayer

The one who ate the brains of animals   presumably
Agreed   Agreed to meet with us

First in the open field
Then in the new wing where blood tested positive
His tested positive again
An incomplete report
And garbled   What is   Air   untouchable air   *Fire your aide*
He thought the lesions disappeared
When he prayed   sir
He gave incriminating facts to foreign journalists

That is our concern   The blowback
The rumors play on rumors
Enlivening the lesser embassy receptions
The usual scotch and pyramids
Of grapes and cubed Gruyère
And *we pulled out   Senator   You were pushed   sir*

By prayer   He told the press   prayer
Nothing to do with you

III

Why assume I am as you are when I am my own *Lord*
I am nothing to do with you
I give myself men circling
Men who cherish secrets in the reassuring hole
They are wives of rain   A fluid follows
Buttocks dripping rain
Good to see their hours alive   O see them see them alive

*

The Worker.   *One could deny all this or intervene*

When they summon the dead
When idiots like him infect their underlings in prayer
The Seer.   *One could no more admit*
Their authority than laugh
At toxic waste they bring like demented children demanding praise

*

The Poet.   *One could sing of armed men*

Or sing the rumor wars
Where folly arms each in turn   and fools will sing of it

Someone's lawyer closed his eyes
His last advice whispered
In the Senate hearing room   and as he leaned back
His client echoed   *What I did*
Savoring syllables
In the exuberant god voice he used on his dogs
What I did is indivisible from
National security

Amor patriae   *I pity those hungering for revelations*
Scapegoats   labs in outer space
He assumed he was absolved
With the sun brightening wet air   when his sneer made them laugh
Blithe propaganda
For a future round about

And rising as a rumor in fields without end
If souls first wake escaping wounds

Upon the Losses of Her Lovers

NOVEMBER 1996

Bill lost, or was it Bob? By now
I might admit their love of power
Almost equals mine. My Bill,
No longer liberal or thin,
With tennis partners, body guards,
Self-serving arguments . . .
He was so much like Bob in bed
Or zany Ronny. Memory
Prefers these sweet displacements.
Who asked for pity and admiration?
Was it Bill, ambitious Bob?
Or was it me, chronicling
His promises, his absences,
In pursuit of my happiness.

The Feather President

THE HISTORY

Unfit as any man to represent them,
He declared, "If none be fit or fated to it,
Why not let the dissonance be mine?
For I, no less felonious, felicitous,
Lo, I, no longer weak of wit and vile,
Dreamed in elevated rhetoric
That, like the lifted face my wife survived
Was calculated to inspire. It did.
I did. I gave my life to public service . . .

Thanks to my miraculous staff, and wife."

THE FIRST BOOK OF HOLINESS

He heard his manager warming up the crowd with his past: His years in local government, his bills, his brother's illnesses, his father's death. How like his manager to add a whiff of Christianity to legal wrangling. His case against The Blue Cross was more than local news when he won.

And was the weather hopeful, the wind drifting off with clouds? His manager left the platform, leaving them to hope below the trees, and hope in sunlight filtered through the summer trees.

Then flares rose, a glow of scarlet, white, blue light, and smoke hung high above faces tipped to the sky. "Happy Days Are Here Again," and sky again and God again: The bands arrived with brave amateur renditions of the old songs, the feathered things; they wafted up the shore, as far up the blue hill as he could see.

But The Blue Cross covered nothing now. Bodies were uncovered. Bodies were uncovered in the field. That was what The Blue Cross did to the land.

He could hear the people breathing on the hill for jeopardy, a chill assimilated, expecting his extremity, head injury, a severed arm, expecting in it some security. "Then they tore my legs off and threw them over there." Politics acted on him as salvation did on others. Hope. Deeds, mysterious companions.

THE INAUGURAL ADDRESS

The land was ours before we were the land's.
The land before the land was ours was land,
But still unstoried, artless, unenhanced,
Unpossessed; if unimagined, unpossessed.
The land vaguely realizing westward,
As people vaguely realized aggression.
We found out that it was ourselves.
And then what story? Or collateral success?
Ask not what your country can do for you,

Ask what happiness you will pursue.

THE FIRST UNEXPURGATED BIOGRAPHY

He took another chicken wing; his least favorite, "Satan's Chicken Polka-Dates" in Phoenix, what with all the good paprika-dusted pitless dates. The podiums smelled of chicken wings.

"Chicken à la campaign," his wife recoiled. When you give your wife syphilis, you forgive her eccentricities. She wore a Paris hat allegedly from Texas. Feathers were too whimsical for Texas, and he needed Texas votes. Fowl joke on him. Chicken wit. She smiled through every heavy potluck chicken supper: The lactating nymph he loved:

the oral tradition. Call it his reward for rural fund-raisers, the chickens cut up, curried, stewed, souffléd for intimates; for crowds, whole fowls "Kansas Fried"; "Savannah Chicken." Volunteers

slathered sauce on chicken breasts, sleek with Millard Fillmore's barbecue, vermouth and vinegar. Then "Pearl's Delmarva Cacciatore"; "Kentucky Fried" or smothered, "Illinois Style"; Long Island à la king for breakfast; lunch, Tandoori; Mole; "Rosemary Mustard Wings"; in Queens, livers; chickens chopped with onions, eggs; a catalog of

fowls, a republic of chickens trumpeted with pleasure forward led, with hope, with salt, with paper bags of family money, unlimited informal contributions. And the bands played faster, the people nearly festive,

bandying about tomorrow. He heard his manager warming up the crowd with his past. And when assassins found him and fired, the Paris hat rose in marvelous, unpremeditated wind, and white and blue feather fragments pirouetted with the sound of it, waving in perpetuity, as the people ran away.

WHERE ARE THEY?

That was not the legacy he wanted,
Not feathered hats proliferating, not
IN GOD WE TRUST on coins during a war.
The blue fox urinating on the hill
Threw angels off the scent of his remains.
And so they hurried on, the feathered things,
And reached for any representative,
Filling their robes with rain, the still-warm rain,
For God was happy when he made the rain.

"Other than that, Mrs. Lincoln, did you like the play?"

Did you hear the one about a widow who paused over lilacs in a blue glass horn? She stood above the fragrance, until it finally overwhelmed the wit she took to be aggression, aggression not her own but some assassin's. She was safe among her silences, lilacs, humorless, reading in the evening of the President's assassination.

"If four more die, will we get a week off from work?"

His manager amassed the first public archive of assassination humor, and though he loved the jabs, fun squibs, puns, jokes, retold, he mumbled, sounded witless; worse, sad. "Wit, a coward's grief."

HO HO HO HO HO

After the assassination, his successor sent the soiled Lincoln back to Michigan for repair. Little of the original car remains at the White House, but four aluminum brake drums that flared. And no, you are not the first to ask. The interior is preserved by Ford Motor Company and available for viewing on specified summer afternoons.

The drive is not as long, as horrible, as you expect, and children will remember presidents on wheels, pulled by sparrows, party hacks, reined and bitted, swift, a shiver, beautiful,

And waking somewhere new, wherever meaning calms.

Puritans brought lilacs to America,
Brought the nonchalance of angels,
Launching forth, knowing what profiteth the soul:
The salt; the burial of failures at sea. Ah,
Smell the land as they did in the air
Before they saw it: elderberries, sassafras,
Something like a red cedar.
                              "Dearly Beloved,
The island smells like home."
Though *"home be nowhere but the soul"*

Was added necessarily and then forgotten.

(UNFINISHED)

They saw birds call the distant warmer air the happiness pursued. Closer now, the barking floating flocks; the snarling last surviving giants, white in lilac and the hour in which the soul withdraws. Will they hover? Will the happiness, the sane and sacred luxury? OK, OK, so call it all a dark conceit!

And now it was the child listening to what was never asked of her who entered the morning in a shiver, chanting "happiness, happiness," (inherited)

And ran as far up the blue hill as she could see.

Upon the Bed-Trick Played on Jack

Why, all the souls that were were forfeit once.

—*Measure for Measure,* 2.2

MARILYN [*as* ISABELLA]: *I had rather give my body than my soul—*
        [*as* MARILYN]: Some lines come more easily than others.

I read this to Jack over the telephone.
Exhale on "my"? Inhale "body"? Hundreds,

He had a thousand comic "vigorous" breaths
To recommend . . . for *me,* as Isabella,

Dear nun! Frigid, misfit, desperate.
   [*as* NORMA JEAN]: I know her, know the dream that God—absent

God alone—loves me—*God, I wanted to learn!*
    [*as* MARILYN]: Why did he laugh? Finally, they all laugh.

    [*as* ISABELLA]: "I had rather—" drain off memories, if mercy
    [*as* MARILYN]: Is defined as high colonics . . . or champagne

Or servicing the presidential prick?
    [*as* ISABELLA]: The rest—the soul rumored into farce—predicted.

*

JOHN [*as* JACK]: God, her ass, a veritable New Fron—tée—ah!
She in town—then Jackie "insists" we catch
Meh-shah fah Meh-shah . . .
Fun as Communion; we took it from rank bastards
Who spent their nights rejoicing at the baths.
    [*as* ANGELO]: *And she will speak most bitterly and strange.*
  [*as* PRESIDENT]: I remember. The one about a great man's failings.
Absurd deceptions, in the name of romance.

[*as* JOHN]: I constructed romances on a man's health,
On "vigah" from amphetamines and cortisone.
The pain—my own parody of faith—
Was used to humanize me: God's good sport
Reduced to ergonomic rocking chairs.
She asked other men to throw my son in the air.

*

JACQUELINE [*as* MARIANA]: *I have known my husband, yet my husband*
Knows not that ever he knew me.
[*as* JACQUELINE]: For I was Marilyn, when Marilyn
Cooed his "happy-ever-aftering."

[*as* JACKIE]: His sadly perfunctory rhapsodies were rude,
[*as* JACQUELINE]: Were all the same to me, since I was always
Mary, Angie, Grace, Giancana's Judith,
His growing underclass of compulsive lays.

Liquor, lighting, hand-painted Paris scarves
Mattered more, in a husband's education,
Than any woman's luscious incarnation.

Oscar Wilde: "To become the spectator
Of one's own life is to escape the suffering . . ."
I tried, Love, and Damn, but love survived.

"Worship of Venus"

After Titian

Naked boys
Swarm for acres, warm across the ancient field.
Some are drowsy by the cut pine. The others play,

Picked clean, whirling as they wave to her.

Why wait for them to hurt themselves? Let the winged ones
Scream in her pollinated air. She made them all,
Made them male

And small, and she
Will keep them small. Kisses this refrain. Her nipples
Harden, nudge the slightest gown damp with milk.

After all, it is the hour for her hair.

Acolytes approach, carrying combs and oils
Flecked with gold, over the scattering boys.
Perform appreciation:

Nod to orchestrated
Pampering, massage . . . She loves fingers, lathered,
Cradling in foam her brain, her infinity.

Let those around her change. Another birth meant nothing

To her body, her sullen pleasure stepping from a bath.
She turns her mirror, as an encore, on her thighs.
Her oldest aims—

Babies make
Their mothers laugh—an arrow at her. Executed laugh.
The others settle at her feet. Grin, alas.

Inadequate accomplices. Poor accessories.

When he drops his arrow, approaches—Too old for this,
She sighs, accepts one kiss, wetting his brow with kisses,
Young wine.

She dribbles wine
On his testicles, soothes her favorite son, his folded skin.
She holds him, holds the knife, and brings it through him. Wine,

More wine, is dabbed on the throbbing, and his tongue,

Crouched and dry in the pink-dark . . . She loves his silence,
Holy as the stained grass and the pollinated air.
The winged ones scream

In ignorance.
She leans, like a horse rearing, over him,
And nurses him, worships his amnesia.

He is adorable in the morning, when horizontal yellows

Stretch and disappear in cinnabar, in blood
That colors acres, warm across the ancient field.
Tomorrow charms.

After the Declaration of Independence

"Yet even then, Desire was dependent
        On what ought to be.

                    *

We 'are, and of right ought to be FREE
        AND INDEPENDENT.' Instead,
We hold ideas of what ought to be.

        We ought to be enlarged
By declaration, identity distended
        By it, sound-engorged.
We ought to have, to have and hold, to hold
        Here in our hands, a minute,

A lover's shoulders, damp, spinning slowly
        In Virginia heat.

                    *

And if 'to have' simulates 'to be,'
        As it does here,
Then we are only what we own again,

        Not our weird desires,
Anxieties about Desire, smeared across
        An unresistant world.

                    *

Are they as representative of us
        As property, when taken

For identity, when all else fails?"

                    *

        He moved his lips alone,
Below the acrid fragrance of imported trees.
        Hear a serenade
Of ice on glass, echoing glass, ice,

A distant violin,
A solipsism that could pass for Independence?

*

He turned, walking on,
Enamored of his contradictions, arguing,
    "Yet even then Desire

Was Independent, or could be, ought to be,
    At least as an idea:

*

As gossip on an orgy at Monticello,
    Where maidenheads, torn,
Bled, and grape seeds were spit on the residues of semen.

    Gossip on abrasions repeated.
Someone slapped to inaugurate pleasure,
    Whipped in the telling; why?
Pleasure in the telling? The whipping? Or
    More alive in alarm

When unenlightened? That was one idea,
    Before Independence yielded,
In the leisure it requires, to Dependence,
    And opposites merged."

*

He loved her these years after his wife—

    Evenings, he left
His library; tonight after he opened the end
    Of revised Palladio,
Touching Doors and Windows; walked late,
    Touching his serpentine wall,

Wet moss; humidity made him tired.
  Then another door
Touched the light below it. It ought to be
  Open to him at once.
It was. See his tired progress through

    Her green cotton shift?

      *

But what did she declare? Independence—
  "More, there"—by degree?
The way he was with her boys "was progress,
  Wasn't it? A world

In the big house with hiding places,
  Heat; why not?"

      *

Because more could be imagined, honey,
  Like a' ice bucket
Bust his . . . "another bad afternoon

    Mopping that up . . ."
She slapped him, fit him to her. This, to him,
  A curious stimulus.

      *

Only inferiors believed in equality
  After they were conceived.

He stood by one of several windows he designed.

      *

    Her idea of Independence
Gave more dignity to her long day
  When it was overcome.

      *

And he admitted, in ever tighter circles,

Choosing foreign virgins,
Anuses, animals, dependents, indifferent to—no,
Pain—the pain the point,
The pain distracted from a history
No one could display,

And were they not very tired by now
When magnolia petals
Through the window trembled in Virginia moonlight
Tipping over stars
Like a gray toy boat snagged with a branch a boy

Found and broke in the finding?
Distractions slow and bless the evening with fatigue,
Everlasting fatigue.
We are and ought to be united in fatigue.

                    *

The mind bows down

Before it, hope usurped, et cetera,
Gradual as shadows
Stunting leaves. Desire changes, why not,
It seems natural,
Back to an idea, and alien.

✳ ✳ ✳

Variations on a National Air

Treason never knew you.

—Emily Dickinson, 1868

"Change was in the air," Mr. Clemens boasted
With journalists he brought to the President's daughter's tea.
"I have made the name of officeholder rogue.
Born & reared 'poor white trash,'
I have clung to my native instincts, & done
Every small mean thing my eager hands could find to do . . ."

This she quoted to her last unmarried friend back home.
Not for sympathy from Tennessee, but say,
"Would you? Would you defend a father who never knew you?"

Her arguments against impeachment
As a conspiracy of sin passed for wit among Radical Republicans.

Hear the titillating venom remembered as a fact?

Even she tried in her way, through devotion, to feel immense,
When Mr. Clemens kissed her hand.
Exciting laughter. She did not dare rebuke them.
Father needed her again. "Was he pardoned?" "Who remembers?"
"Does acquittal sound familiar?" "For what?"
What secretly recorded confession by the gate?

"The optical illusion of invading Communists?"
Journalists, to pass the time, a hundred years,
A thousand, a hundred thousand fund-raisers in Virginia,

Wrote obscenities across the party list of past contributors:
CEOs from pharmaceuticals;

Philanthropic widows; withered billionaire Iranians;

The frightened lobbyist Monsanto "retired."
Was he the one who sent peaches the night the President resigned,
The "new baby donuts" he engineered?
And was he seated for his trouble next to last year's star?
Or down among the wives of possible ambassadors
Whose anecdotes devolved to recipes:

Cobbled peaches, cognac, ginger snaps,
Ingredients exchanged, like Sudan for Afghanistan,
"Not India," "Naturally," murmured near him

In a garden under metal-lined umbrellas.
The corporate implications of impeachment

Were protected from the other side's surveillance.

An hour went by, didn't it, and why not another now,
A flute of peach Asti with dessert?
He groaned. He knew, for all his contributions in the past,
He would never be given even
An inessential nation like Peru.
He might as well go back to Louisville.

Then the former first lady saw him and walked him to the gate.
"She mentioned me to George for Nepal,"
He said, when anyone asked back home.

Smell her Shalimar, and when a breeze swanned around,
Smell the peaches, heavy on the newer trees.

"Why didn't you impeach—?" "Did I dare —?"

The Senator rolled his trousers up
Until his mistress intervened, "So soon after Nixon?"
"Reagan?" "You are old," his daughter wounded him.
She loved her long investment in his death.
"Sharper than a serpent's plume," he fumbled,
Crumbling at last. Meaningless! Nothing at last!

They circled his infirmities; fiends! Confusion!
No! He is not a hound dog sniffing up
Volunteer Cordelias eager to play the Fool.

I have known a daughter's silence, insistent,
Selfish, self-protective, ostentatious in the name of love.

A fool, when President would do. Deity too.

I never dared adapt to the deity in me, the music, the—
"Who cares? And who cares who cannot ever care?
I have labored not to care," he winked at journalists
Who never never never never never care.
He sang, each to each, lingering in humidity,
Combing his hair red and brown between appearances.

I heard him ride ahead of waves of spent azaleas,
Picturesque and inaccessible, interrupting,
Nay, entirely rejecting, the majesty imagined for myself.

"Then why hang on?" Journalists began, coming, going.
"'Come, let us goe,' or you alone, go; change is in the air."

"Here, there, and everywhere,

A peach-colored twilight." "A fair thing in a fatherland."
Another last hurrah in history
I heard and hurried down past the trees, the intricate
Persistences: violence within the gate.
"Does it close?" Shut the door. I shut the door.
Reason not the thrill! if anyone agrees to survive.

Crazy Horse in Wannsee

JANUARY 1942

They hunted me in prairie grass,
Hunted me by the falls and falling
Cliffs, the coneflowers where the flash
Weeds bend west to the pine ridge.
So long they hunted me that when
My one brother was brought to the fort,
They saw my face in his surrender,

His forgiveness. That was not my face.
And that was not a good day to die,
Not in the Drying Grass Moon.
Who will say what happened in
The dream? Will I? Will you, friend?
Will we let the Germans tell us
When the wind is friendlier?

And will it be a fiction like forgiveness,
A Luftwaffe wafer fiction,
A self-forgiving crucifiction:
Forgiveness, the final solution?
Who will say the friends lost
Will not return? The buffalo return
And may be happy in Berlin.

The boulevards are muffled grass.
The horse paws and darkens snow,
Dancing on linden branches, shadows,
Crazy in the greasy grass,
Snorting and falling in love again.
Who will say if I had their weapons,
I would lay them in winter grass?

I Saw in Late November Pumpkins

And I carried on my shoulders pumpkins
Up Broadway, on the omnibus, and in the back, a young man,
Young to me, rocked back and forth with only the window,
Fluttering trees, the wind
To steady him with brief comparative softness, "wilt."

I heard his "wilt," "wilt" repeated to the storefronts and
Horses tethered, rumps, traffic-aft; "wilt,"
Said he to the Old Bowery Theatre, the sign
For comedies on kings. "Wilt," and wilt
His cry come unto me?

And what to answer "wilt," such "wilt" he knew, riding
The city as I did, the weight of a rude imposing dawn upon him
That was mine. His face I carry and his eyes, as eyes
On sweet potatoes, going farther into their fiber,
Sweet, sweet, sweet potatoes:

"Let the sky rain potatoes," said I laughing, and
Marked his stubble, an afterthought of manliness,
The ruddy wild fear I know, and knew to hide,
From the beginning; mine.
"I know thee not, old man." He turned to the window,

Rocking, endlessly rocking; horses waited as we passed, and sky.
I think of him now with the pride privacy rewards
And know rewards do come to those unprepared for joy.
I saw what he was, what work
It was to be alive,

A solitaire, poor boy, proud butternut, so
He will squash, and live to squash again, a once and future squash.
O my soul, I do love
The sound surrounding me that hounds him out, the rocking ache
I was, wilted, carrying pumpkins home in late November.

*

Now is the autumn of my appetite,
When affairs stand as smaller separate spheres,
As the pumpkin's blond leaf,
Once like the orange-gray pumpkin opulence, confidence,
Firm and fat enough for a boy's idea of heaven.

Concoct a pumpkin cock and cocky breast bravado,
Merry multitudes of sumptuous buttocks;
Lovers of girth, of lusty crenellations, seeds.
Is she not generous in her obesity?
Is he not radiant,

Inflated for significance? Very well, inflate, and
Ferry me over a
Range of orange, arc to arc, a tempo of hills at intervals,
And see that inward, inward, inward is its own reward,
As the day is completed by reminiscences as friends.

"Precious Things"

Here the man stoops nights, he
Stomps empties, you know what I'm sayin, to gather
      Trash night Cokes and Old Milwaukees, Coors, Stroh's,
          All the glad good cheer manqué.
          "Blame not my lute."

      Damn near dead, huntin tin, aluminum, partsa metal scrap.
That shopping cart to cobblestones, not a wang dang doodle
          Pothole blues,
          And not my lute, my dear.
The alley partsa this part, lit,

An wif hisself, say: "'PRECIOUS THINGS—
      Hold my rooster, hold my hen, / Pray don't touch my Grecian Bend.'"
          And night be now a shine.
          Over to the hospital, men buy metal,
      And you might say too

If you had blood rejected, you remember where.
A wind again interrupts. The man
          Straightens, standing, "Wohw,"
      Way too fast *"oh shit,"* and all the cans together,
          A very heap of trembling,

Will not bring what a rusted tossed compressor will, copper & all.
Deep in a Waste Management bin,
          The luck of a chunk a change.
          And cans, they spill aside,
      For the precious enter first and ride away.

A shining sound commends not hope, or enterprise, or charity,
      And not my lute, my dear.
      Damn close to the noble peasant who endures.
           A wind again interrupts. Be now a
Shining place. Night be now a shining place. A praise sound.

Worship of Mars

The golden age of ammunition continued:
Force whenever possible, now with fewer arguments,
And none expected
                    in the years to come.
                                        Drifts of Japanese
        Anemones, tall and double white
        Perennials, nodded imperceptibly, then bowed
To visitors from
                    Rome, Rio, Harare,
                                    Kuala Lumpur.
        They traveled light with ceramic guns, fooled,
        Predictably, the border apparatus, the poorly paid guards
Who beckoned them on,
                    amiably on
                                        through secured corridors.
        And now, down the changing coast,
        When they landed, bathed, gathered near him, for his first
Shot, the welcome shot,
                    the one the footman
                                        recognized, he fired,
        And the dreamy scent he patented
        Crowded scented air with scented gunpowder; fired
"Catharsis," his first
                    gunpowder; fired
                                        "Winter Sandalwood";
        "War Is Kind," the scent like his cologne.
        Their pleasures envied his in the open air.
Their emulation,
                    his domination,
                                        like the meal he chose,
        The falling langoustine soufflés,
        Were common transformations gone awry. You saw it too.

The footman, a farm boy, mascot (*Quel* hoot!)
Ran then with hampers
Of cold fowl and raspberry-cocoa ices
Nestled in silver and glass,

And such a pity, in retrospect,
That our nouveau riche—
With their vestigial envy
Of European minds

(Enlightened myopia, and luncheons
On the long west lawn;
Drinks under a timidly festive
Wisteria shade)—neglect

Or fetishize their bodies, as "style."
All rumors of a puritan gene,
True; and true the "pure" romances
Among the medicated

And morally repugnant elite.
"A philosophy of action?"
"On a bed of chronic fatigue?"
"Nasty recombinant genes . . ."

He watched the footman pile the bowls and glass too high
And knew he could not resist a missing tooth, a bruise;
A submissive gallop. See the dear boy

Fly with a dripping tray? Another "improving American"?
And birds left the ancient fountain, one last peck,
Before they flew off, irrelevant,

Dripping on the perfect grass, on massed white anemones,
"Venus's Tears," that flower of grief in China.
The pleasures of domination began,

God, how many years ago? When he was "it," Chinese, Japanese,
The "it" boy enemy from afar? If slaughter needed,
Why not him? Ah brutal will!

He ran, his cousins yelling at him optimistic battle cries.
One fell, remember; he turned, on the scream; a body squirmed
In the distance, a different cry.

Then others running back, smaller in crisis, one calling "Ma—"
For his aunt, dear old aunt, her mouth open as she ran,
Her blue skirt on his mouth,

The blood taking the cloth into it, and taking her too.
And how the game ended: No one running over where he was,
To say he won. *Quel* hoot!

> His aunt was kissing him goodbye,
> The twilight on the couch,
> The color of her hair. "Resistances,
> Not acquiescence, arouse."

> She laughed superbly and left, and he
> Continued, indolent, "Cruelty
> Impresses. People need a scare.
> They want to be used,

> Afraid, beaten up; need
> Pain; they need to dread."
> A genital chanting, dear shadow,
> A hunger, remembered, spread.

Others will submit with a shudder. "Blood—"

"Is he bleeding yet?" A few were leaving, "the less courageous."

"To be expected."

"He persisted," "when

he who penetrates—"

"Arrived." "Enemies invigorate."

"They speed the blood; the minor ones clean it." "A benefit of war."

"Like wealth." The rest laughed.

"Wealth, like envy—"

"Wonders of the world."

"You will never change your life; why try?"

Days of 1948

"My dear,

        Canvassing, door-to-door,
No end to the nights. Next year, next
Week, say to me, never canvass again.

Men, women, they beg through doors,
Beg through a little crack like a
Little understanding rejected.

Would not sign because of jobs,
Would lose my job. The harm dreamed.
And hours hearing the wives explain
They fear God. People are easily afraid.

Republicans, Democrats, both call,
Swearing to these tired people,
Christ, you're registered a Communist!

Just because they sign petitions,
Sign for one candidate besides
'The average man's average man'
And class, 'gluttons of privilege,'

Republicans. People are easily afraid.
Priests, reporters, ask, Are they
Afraid yet? Republicans, Democrats

Ask, Are they afraid? Funny.
Funny, Lenin's words come back
When tired as tonight, *Patience,*
Irony. I miss your Lenin, all

Promise, the long view. Politics
Without discipline is gossip,
Like that softy Béla Bartók,

Making 'an olive of himself,'
Singing, *Labor, that's La Boré,*
Under 'the martiniest debutantes.'
That is Paul's kind of comedy.

Mine is largely Bela Lugosi,
Hungarian parodies of force.
Always he jokes, I have the letter:

His concerts are a *propaganda,*
If he sings a Russian lullaby.
Problem lullabies, he underlines,
A pit of lullabies, a snake pit.

There goes the vice-presidency,
The service I would do the state.
They know it. They know I serve,

Speaking now of race hatred.
You know we both are cheered
By solemnities, resistances,
The dream of control. No more of that.

Did you grasp his testimony
Before the Judiciary Committee?
Or that jackal Senator, serious,

Robeson wants to be a martyr.
Maybe we ought to make him one.
The news will make you plotz,
I trust, on his behalf. Or laugh.

I called him, afterwards, from work.
People will confuse Progressives,
Communists. It's Truman's plan.

America is hysterical. 'Truman's
"Womb-suffering"?' says I.
'What a democratic hell
To give 'em: "Womb-suffering."'

He laughed that big laugh, a sound
Like some dogma on survival
I am not afraid to need.

Let's walk, he said; the nights walked,
Like in the old days. We haggled
Shlock, like 'swing,' like 'Meet the Press,'
Like proud, blond, movie-Nazis.

Some days the world proves how mean it is.
Some nights Toscanini on the radio,
The little unshakable night music.

Patience, irony, my dear."

Work Song

A man bites his briefcase handle.
I catch his privacy
   One slow winter morning
In a wet subway car,
As though it happened once
   And never happened again.

With a hey nonny no, and a dollar to go!
  So poor, yourself to blame,
The days were never worth remembering.
   This life is most brave.

A man bites his briefcase handle,
As the car sways with bodies
   Nodding, tucked in scarves,
Exogamous courtesy.
Winter kindness: indifference,
   The sun biting the earth.

With a hey nonny no, and a dollar to go!
  So poor, yourself to blame,
The days were never worth remembering.

A man bites his briefcase handle,
Knowing the world to come
   Will bless its witnesses.
One by one, their wildness,
Worthless; work hosts worth.
   Bite I "work"!—Stop there!

With a hey nonny no, and a dollar to go!
So poor, yourself to blame,
The days were never worth remembering.
This life is most brave.

The *Et Tu* Etudes

Et tu, Brute?

—Julius Caesar

I

My grander hours are elaborated by musicians,
     On and on in the next room.
And you, pretending to listen, nap,
Unguents dripping from your fine hair.
     A pretty boy tiptoes up
     With better wine, blended,
As you like, with honey and seawater and myrrh.

II

Never underestimate the malice of little minds.
They peck open what they can,
               fretful, hopeful,
     And leave like birds flying south with followers.
What else is new? The weather overwhelms, and you agree.
     Agree, agree,
           a cheap duplicity I love.

III

     Did they touch my cape after I took their land?
I came, I saw, I conquered.
Intimacy is not the aftermath.
     Let us leave desperation to assassins.

And thank the magistrates
And so on: "The most courageous people, because
           Continuously at war."

And you: "Shall I compare that to your courage?
Compare the northern star,
           The roughened summer days
To your courage?" Flattery is a tedious revenge.

IV

I baffled you, when I refused the crown.
           My arms reaching out for you then, dear boy,
Naturally. And you somehow accepted the assault.

V

           All I did for you:
The oval circuses, the lower seats rebuilt in stone.
           Innumerable criminals dismembered for you.
           Races: Horses trotted out, kicking the mica flecks
From sand like falling volatile stars I named for you. And you
           Loved the crushed horses.
           All you loved I knew.

VI

           I pity you. Pity, like regret,
           Adds a piquancy to leisure. And you, my epigrams,
Intercept regret.

VII

Downstage, the morning train to Washington, D.C.

Fills with the middle class, assimilated blond blacks
And plucked whites, who lean on latent sleep.
"You said it." "Umm-hmmm." "Get me some a that."
And nodding off, a head bangs the window, wakes:
What is it, Thursday, July, and you run for the train,

Holding a tie and coffee; find the last seat
Behind the sleeping clerks and data analysts,
Refugees from mergers; find despair, you argued
Later, looking back, a child's procrastination.
I agreed: All the world's speed is rejected

In despair, though fantasy provides a destination.

VIII

How inspiring would I be in a crown?
A gold frond rimmed in emeralds; not too many, I think. I think
A graphic reference to my constellation would delight the women.
                    Fix the pink serpent's
                    Saliva, diamonds,
In the back. I think they like a brave man better from the back.
                    Praise their modesty.
                    Add modest onyx
For my triumphs, sardonyx for attributes. And you said,
                    Innumerable.

IX

He left your "message." Treason. It was treason.
And you—where did you buy him?
      The tenth duckbrained slave supposed to "free" you,
          Your legs in the air,
A signature position, a minor nibbling thrill.

      I will yawn, guffaw,
Haw, haw, when you are dragged down the market road,
      Your wishfulfilling prick,
          Rammed in your dead mouth.
Satirists will make of mutilation a sacrament.

X

Then lunch hour, walking up the aisle and back
With bread, if you remember, and roses, circuses, THINGS.
THINGS "glazed with rain / Water," the vision THING.

And you, when you came not to bury but to praise me,
      With nothing on my conduct, my genius,
My latest evening-colored cape, no dismissing
      Epilepsy for exceptional eyes . . .
You said, "We don't like martyrs. Socrates, Horace.
      Never bought that bourgeois resignation THING.

We don't like resignation. Or the Lorca THING:
      The beatific frowns of the Old Left.
They were living in shadows of themselves.
      Imagine living in shadows of yourself,
And dubbing them for dialogue, for the figures
      You came and saw and thought were THINGS."

Am I among the ones who beg to be a THING?
You will murder some THING, a "white chicken" THING.
And as I am, so will the world "BE-THING'D."

XI

    And you stood by the fire. Music followed,
Wiggling points, smoke,
Flute, heat, sputtering low,
Like inferior arrogance.
    A mood you considered democratic.
    A scene: BROODING ON YOUR MEN.

A sigh. They wanted a sign,
Diagonals in ash: What were the odds of doom now,
"When the dawn lay meek in rain . . ."
    You know the slop they want and
Meals of corn and vinegar.
Will you point them on to die? Where is the boy with wine?

    Come here. I have over here
The paste of flamingo brains,
Have the salted congery
Of conger eels, fattened on living slave-meat you love.
    Have Sicily; insist on it,
    And military caprice
Becomes the civility you love, as much as I do, my love.

XII

And you and I had a history, when history
Was fellow feelings falling into place, and war.
You knew conspirators agreed on the hour.
My habits were figured and refigured
As trophies of intellect: Logic rationing
The rage they evidently purified together.
In them, I saw myself years ago,
So alive with enemies. Enemies,
The vivid monuments I visited alone.

Battles in another part of the field,
In green light, were the one consolation,
As clouds moved over them, undefined,
An emanation to no end. No end to it,
No end to that uncertainty: That time
When doubt was thought, and thought, a cloud.
A mere cloud-boy, whose philosophy was peace,
Was vague as any girl with premonitions: Cloud.
No pressure, pleasure, edge. My will be done.

There may be a time when nothing consoles,
But that would be the last consolation,
The local oddity. No balm required or wounds.
No grander hours, no proof of them, like grief.
The evening now is odd and green.
The evening train is full and full of sleep.
We are larger when asleep and warm
And warm when we arrive. Here we are.
The evening air collects our entertainments.

✳ ✳ ✳

White Bottom Blues

I done showed y'all my black bottom
You ought to learn that dance.

—Gertrude "Ma" Rainey, 1928

GIRL: Give me, anywhere's around, the lowest room.
Anywhere's around, the lowest room.
Give me anywhere's around the lowest room.

CHORUS: —Ma done showed y'all her black bottom.
Is that the best you got to show? Ain't no particlar
Bottom's dream, oblivious as joy.—Ma, you helpin her?

—She'll learn.—She stings not, neither do she stomp.
GIRL: Humor me. He said I was his Great Depression. Hon,
I CRASHED! Worked my buttered butt to gleaming. Chump

Burlesque for pocket change, on my knees, Pa. Ha!
Abstract enough for boys in the back room?
They want a BRA & PANTIES matched. OFF'D? How'm I doin?

MAN [*spoken, as to* MA]: *Ah, do it. Do it, honey!*
Look out now, you's gettin kinda rough, girl! You bet' be
Yourself, now, careful, now, not too strong, not too strong, honey!

GIRL: Every Great Depression needs a Star-Spangled Banner.
Every misery, a thrill. I know a bomb, she's burstin backstairs,
Got his rocket's red glare. His flag, it's still there.

What do I care? I FEEL GOOD, banged from way back.
CHORUS: —She slums, but lonesome cruisin ain't carousin, ain't
What Ma would do. Ain't assimilated. Mo' appropriated.

Opportune. Asinine in the best of times, and in the worst,
Divin in, ostensible witness blues?—Ain't that.—Worse—
—Let her be.—Ma?—Only so much some can learn.

GIRL: I can learn. Look, a big white bottom, home and brave.
CHORUS: —Humorous. Humorous.—Hush now. Won't matter days.
Don't worry years.—You know she'll have the last word.

GIRL: Lifted up, last, first, MADAM WHITE BOTTOM TO YOU.
Bottom's up! How'm I doin, Ma? MA: You'll learn.
Some folks got to work that hard for someone else's blues.

Complaint of the Poet to Her Purse

Logic is the money of the mind.

—Karl Marx

Marx? If logic is a problematic surplus value added
On to thought (and thought, illogical alone, libidinal
Nerve in droves), then a poem (a thought) has market value
Ever-commensurate with middlebrow salves: *lucidity, goals,*
Ye olde accessible epiphanies. Poor song, I thought, and

Met the market, merging with it, sleek, succinct, market savvy.
Only I collapsed from entrepreneurial "negative capability,"
Neo-mystery, positively incapable of "poetry careers,"
Earnings. *Panic* (market-tested as exuberance) was truth
Yelled: Is money a long-remembered moot rescue fantasy?

My purse is empty, my purse-lipped pudendum, emptied.
O must I patronize myself—divested in toto—to eat?
No one pops out (pater-accomplice, *pis aller*) eager to fund,
Eager to fill—"Deliver me," I wept one awful night, "from
Yawping poverty, parsed personal—*'or elles moot I die'*!"

"Yapping at me?" Hermes laughed. "Sing me your annual yield,
Eh? You hope I come in as income, gross income, fabulized
Security without (mmmmm) scrumptious flesh offerings for me.

Most nihilism bores me. Nihilism is a poor man's ultimatum."
"Objectively? Omnisciently? Money is a woman's sovereignty."
"Narcissism is—" *"Money,"* I thought (this, the logic), "ensures
Each unlikely song beyond accounting—" "Ah, *beyond?* How pure!
Your fear is the money, the impurity, of the mind." Poor song.

Balm

The paramour passes over and another
Has not appeared, not
On the porch, not wandering on the shore, melancholy,
        Joking on melancholy.

And if he "restoreth the soul," was much soul there?

        This to be carved, in dread,
On cedars, clematis, each successive door.
And if the mind argues—

Neither following nor finding another way,

Yet in crossing itself,
The mind restoreth the soul, why should he,
Rising now, appear?
        Sandpipers run over his feet and run away.

Is it good yet? Is it

        A good boy soul the mind restores? Is it good
If on a different night
Light delights a satyred seder, ravishing

Deliverance with bliss?

A different night should portion out the solitude
To cedars, clematis,
And find in this the unity the paramour,
        When he appeared, suggested—

As if to say, in passing, a different night should be

       As liberal—luxuriant—
As the melancholy we knew how to love.
And so it is light that "runneth over" after all,

And all, unsupported by the paramour.

Souvenir of the New World

"The quality of mercy is least strained
When hypothetical in solitude . . ."
Abigail roved the morning grass alone.

Her overly chiasmic God was not amused.
The animals afraid of her kept the leaves musical.

All women would be tyrants if they could.
Abigail held her letter back another week.
"Self-reliance is a manly sorrow . . ."

No. He could hear that wrongly. Or rightly.
"All men would be tyrants if they could,"

She wrote, at peace with his long absence,
Though his sense of it pierced her, his peace.
Something else to tell the evening grass.

Protestant solitude! To each a prayer alone.
Mornings, they had morning walks alone then for heaven.

Little Journeys to M. de Tocqueville's Dump

In democratic communities, each citizen is habitually engaged in the
contemplation of a very puny object, namely himself. . . .
    This appears to me sufficiently to explain why men in democracies, whose
concerns are in general so paltry, call upon their poets for conceptions so
vast and descriptions so unlimited. The authors . . . perpetually inflate their
imagination, and, expanding them beyond all bounds, they not unfrequently
abandon the great in order to reach the gigantic.

—Alexis de Tocqueville

"Explain, explain, explain our failures to us,"

The journalist went on, "as little edifying journeys?"
His moral immensity escaped the city editor,

And the people, whose "concerns are in general so paltry."
His concern was the dump, the mayor's dump, the boats
The mayor welcomed, the turmoil, and millionaires.

Mornings when they docked upwind, dropping waste

From other nations, contraband asbestos, chromium,
Plutonium, plastic residues, the shore disappeared,

And in the night, so did the necessary moon.
"Not physically possible," the governor declared.
He never believed the dump rose to the moon.

"But the smell," said the mayor, "the nothing, not there."
He no longer feared the governor; no, "admired" him.
He admired quantum mechanics in small quantities.
The governor, like a particle in a specific problem,

Never materialized, however isolated, in his mind.
His son did, though, climbing the ever-ripening,
Etceterating dump, clinching his deserved reelection.
The boy should wave into the voters' minds
And propagate the ever-puny light there.

Now the boy admired his father, but he was afraid.
"Bones lie on the dump, aborted gunk, dogs, headless dogs,
So unlimited . . ." The boy wailed louder and was led away.
People saw the mayor's son enter the clattering rot.
And for a long time, he was stepping high over wire,
Crumpled hubcaps, leaking muck, the honk honk honk

Of falling horns. They saw, then, far above them, no boy.

Another boy, any boy, was summoned. Up he went.

"Dumped!" They roared when at once he disappeared.

Even this the mayor justified to the journalist
With the recently discovered drifts of icy excrement,

The lozenges of melted monuments . . .
He wanted to go on but watched the people watch
The governor point beyond the dump to the moon.

"One man's universe is another's talking excrement,"
The mayor shouted at the dying moon.
"And the right boy climbing the finest dump
Surely would sufficiently explain my way. . ."

And so it was the same night he found himself a boy,
A volunteer: the boy who climbed his grandmother's tree.
He was curious, held a make-do branch, and leapt—
Each step, each uncertainty, was, as the others learned,
Music, a random broken fan falling music, hitting a

Silly wicker stool music, fated to trivia music,
Minty dreck. He rose through all the old silver narratives:
A dumped, warped baby grand, the "lady's heroin";
Some lucky yellow-gray travel condoms. Blond foundlings.
He saw the tops of wild walnut trees and crowds
No longer shouting for him. "I disappeared," he thought,

And heard a sound. Another boy? He slipped

Where a part of a boat fell on the mayor's dead son.

He turned under a light wind and heard *Be Thou,*
The sound, whirring awake in the warming rot,

Be Thou, the old behemoth in ludicrous decay,
Loud: *Be Thou A Very Puny Object.* Again,
The second boy, astride a goat, shouted, *Thou—*

No, the small boy shook his head, laughing. Ho ho.
The morning puffed out, puffed the rapid blows,
Blow! *Be Thou* the blow, the richest hour, a rout in dew?
The genius of menace was in its choreography,

Closing in, then not, then closer, inefficient. *Be Thou*
"Me," or be for me a delicious crippled fright.
The second boy retreated, lifted up by crows.
Here the boy feels the way a man must alive:
The silence, a thorn aura, an authority.

Here the man remembers an appetite for silence
And the moon long ago, buried in the dump.
Tourists marveled as he moved across the sky
In moon-colored raiments, a purified buffoon.
The mayor paid him well to approximate the moon,
Yet he did marvel at the market for buffoons.

He launched his paper boats. Down the hill they sailed.

Long ones for fighting, round ones for trade.
The top sails puffed out, *beyond all bounds, gigantic.*

He folded his arms over his eyes, a gesture of flight
That was not liberty, he learned belatedly,
As the dump extended rapidly downwind and beyond.

Poem for the Wheat Penny

1909–1958

O beautiful
The amber the clamor the waves of grain
              The need for animal feed
          And liquor yes the need for heaven

I heard a voice in the midst of beasts say
A measure of wheat for a penny

O spacious
Voice that loafs and voids a day
              A voice numismerized
          Is it love my one

Nation leaning her cheek upon the grain

O love
The penny cried which wheat which voice
              Which night the penny moon
          Shall subsidize the need for heaven

I heard a voice need yes a prop abundance
The measured fat of the wheat the penny-wise

O say
Say the penny-candy prayer
              The dawn a gleaming pile
          Of trampled swords and friends

The coined and counted nice the penny life

"No Stamping or Whistling Allowed in This Comique!"

"Starting from nothing, a negligible animal act.

Bad example: monkey pantomime, with tuba.
Monkey kicks nice baby chimp up prop 'Alps,' right?
Chimp tumbles. Timing fine, also avalanche effect.
Other monkeys yodel, leering, Swiss-like—what Swiss?

Prim, prim from aggravation, prim leer they give
Monkey, now a shepherdess in tights. Get it? No?
You got it. Without a WOW finish, nothing.
Fired, quick before shepherdess had sheep. And millionsa

Cheap props piled under that old sign by the door,
'NO STAMPING OR WHISTLING ALLOWED IN THIS COMIQUE!'
You hada have a shtick patrol for stale shtick.
That would be me, 'pu-lease' police, ha ha. For rot

Begging burial, bombs. I unbooked the booked.
Like a booking should be unbreakable. Who said
From bribing? Bah! By whose? Listen, see:
Jugglers on unicycles up above the best plush seats

Tossing lovely cherry-colored leather balls? Shmaltz,
Gone. Gone professor balancing icebox on proboscis.
Also inherently hilarious bellboy jokes, remember those?
'Hells bells, boy, ring a ding ding.' Reliable punch line?

'Puh-lease.' Never worked west of Chicago. A snore.
Polar bear pallbearers, now that's a WOW finish, see?
Warm 'em up with water nymphs from Indochine,
Then polar bear pallbearers on 'frozen eyeball juice.'

But southa Philly, it haddabe slow, a 12-minute bit.

Who knew? No, the perfect big-time, never. Perfect,
Yes; continuous, yes, but perfecto & continu-o-so? Where?
Every crowd, every town, every night, something screwy.
Dunt believe me, dunt esk! What am I telling you?

Not reliable, not Helen Keller soliloquies.
Not grinning, dancing green bean, Adele's brother,
Chasing Douglas Fairbanks. 'And a fair young bank he was.'
That Grouch! Hey, we're talkin here. Lose the camera.

Is this respectable? Pictures you never mention, no.
Picture Bert Williams, Houdini, Eva Tanquay.
Like I'm punished in this life, you can't picture the beyond?
A joke, right? What am I, talking to myself?

Like I said, *negligible animal act,* but not a bomb.
Like Little Hip, 'Smallest Elephant in the World.'
What a sweetie! Built largest-ever vegetable Venus de Milo
Right before your eyes. And Cupid cantaloupe finale.

Next up, *action,* slapstick, knockabout, wake 'em up:
'The Laughable Irish Sketch, Our DoodleDoo & Bill'
Or 'Teutonic Musical Fluff of the Little Fraud.'
Then *climax:* After Bernhardt, endless one-legged *Hamlets.*

Playlets: Revenge of the fantasy-mensch, in song.
The mother made a play for amnesia; the son,
Their sing-along, 'To Be or Not to Be My Baby,'
People liked. Ophelia zinging many slings and arrows

At his 'What a Rogue and Pleasant Fellow Am I.'

People liked the duel, the skull, the Swedish dialect,
And where Ophelia whines, 'If not now when,
The weddedness is all.' Outrageous fortune! Expensive!
That wedding on a boat, her father mugging to the back row,

'Kisses, straight! With a kiss chaser!' while the couple kiss
A thousand chaste American kisses under the stars.
A number like that, people come back for more.
For a bearded-lady Moses & horses, having parted a sea,

Red chiffon, no less, and cellophane, they bow
Before the curtain after intermission. Then *headliner,* you see
How tough to top all that? Blood backstage, on who to follow
Cuttsheep from Miles Stendish, wit a prolock, wit a heppilock:

'Preeceela: Go hatt, John, dollink—spick frilly!'
Or Alfred Lunt in *Ashes* with the legendary 'Jersey Lily';
Siamese acrobats who sang? The evening not so mishmash, see?
'The Greatest Single Woman Singing Comedian in the World':

The day he moved up the playbill, down the billing,
Terrible! Not the daintiest impersonator, but
The wig like caviar, a pompadour, and barely dressed
In aigrettes, *mishegas.* The market for 'sophistication,'

It ended after the crash. She went on, though, a long time,
Throwing kisses underhand, the sweetly infantile ingenue
She haddabe to make it. She flowed forward, singing,
'I've Got a Style All My Own,' 'In the Good Ol' Summertime,'

All profile on the last note, a voice like iced Pernod . . .

Trembling in a salmon spot, in her attenuated prime.
You could see in the crowd the couples nodding, nudging
One another's arms. Mainly girls thumping seats, a younger
Whoopee, aping in the dark the singer's moves.

Greatest trio in the world: love, heartache, survival.
For growing boys too; fans, manly fans! Fathers, families.
But the managers bumped her for bigger draw. What bigger?
The Vomit Meister, him surely you heard? Huge, colossal,

Bigger-than-Houdini-huge, in London, Paris, Singapore.
Offstage, a kind man, sipping water in the wings.
A fire-eater. OK, stale shtick, but I loved it, him too.
The Vomit Meister swallowed fire and vomited fire.

Swallowed lighter fluid, and vomited fluid and fire and
Fluid and fire and then afterglow of shapely smoke,
A rose-blue plume that rose more voluptuously,
So the papers said, than she did in a dream or when she sang.

I thought she'd die. When the Vomit Meister added music,
I thought she'd die. Bless her heart, out she went,
Perfect hair, perfect feathered gown, perfect the works.
To which she added, this was her demise, a middling Lincoln

Imitation, a bevy of John Wilkes Booths, leaping off the stage.
Live parrots chained here and there in lighted cages
To balconies, to potted greenery, some kinda Christmas shtick.
Parrots shrilled: 'They shot my husband, shot my husband,'

Comic interlude the point. Nailed. Her last appearance,

Last 'Statue of Libido' bit, singing 'God Bless America.'
Poor girl. I thought she'd die. Him? Acquired a choir.
How should I know if she died? A joy backstage. She'd say,
To me she'd say, 'Her WOW finish was never marrying.'

The Vomit Meister briefly 'pursued' her, shall we say.
What happened? What happens to anyone? You tell me
What plays, mass, and bows and disappears in the dark.
The final act I like best: 'The New Local Burlesque

Of *Girls of the Golden West.*' Same in any small town.
As ever, 'powerful cast, educating acts, laughs.'
You laughed at the contortionist's tambourine, you
Son-of-a-gun, her trained doves, real diamond G-string.

But tasteful. Too highclass for hardcore.
Ever see the 'Dancing Shiva' shiksas nude, a pantheon
Of flaunts thrust among the angels people rooting for?
That's something people like, a regular resurrection."

Cheers of the Poet to Her Purse

THE FESTIVAL CHEER

We will consider the cheer.
We will lie in the new grass.
We will add ourselves to rain,
The wet path, movements in the grass, the blowing plums.
We will know ephemeral feasts.
Consider the cheer, the warm drink.
We will add ourselves to the dallying
In late sunlight, quickening days.
And I prepare myself for him with my fingers.
A flock provokes us,
    The washed wings and a rustle in elders,
    Musk in prayer. Prepare myself with fingers,
    Prayer. It is insatiable. Wet
    Bowers dissolve in gold, shiver as he passes.
    The gold grapes shiver,
        And the ice-green olives on the little trees.
        The cloud approaches, gold
        In the garden, licking gold the leaves.
        He prepares, I approach him.
        Consider the cheer
    A medium of exchange:
    A taste for consummation,
    Congenital and cheered.
    We will flock to the elders in the garden.
    We will flock to the wet path
And the subtle fruit. The fingers cheer
The hourless hours, ours, and purr the bowels
And the door in thankfulness.
The belly cheer. The welcome drink purrs, dear love,
As poets fill the grass.

But it was inevitable that as the years passed,
It was all devalued.
And city poets, in a stupor of anger,

In defensive harmony,
Argued, "We will praise mediocrity
In exchange for praise. And keep accounts
       Of favors, of perks, blurbs, plugs, pubs.,
       Remunerations, renown. Compared to these,
       Cheer is a minor drunken delusion,
             Vomiting gold. Green. Something like that."
             And then the pain he expects and I prepare
             Is a substitute exuberance,
An aberrance for stimulus.
What else, after all, could we do to one another?
What else devalue? Students flock to us,
Provoked, bruised, aroused, aroused, confused,
And we will pass along resentments and sneer,
The nasty bits, nostalgia for bitterness.
             It is a negative lubricity we spread.
             And fuck them, fuck the students,
             In their loneliness, their nervous arrogance:
       The boy playing piano with his prick,
       The girl adding high notes with her fanny.
       They are wild in their confusion to please us,
A feast of pleasuring children
We take for their father's inadequate praise.
What has he done for us lately, what favors?

Commerce is not, as we expected,
A sublimated carnival, but work to grotesque
Souls—a sad sad goal.

THE CHEER REGAINED

A fair amount was left to us on the hill,
So long as we accepted sacrifice:

The small goat eyes of the virgin, the boy,
The boy, no longer one of us, the one
They led along multitudes, and master flutes
Lifted to the sky. And the shouts

We added added us to sacrifice,
Now his belly slits, now
Thrown on the swept-together shaved evergreens.

And we shouted in the whirling ash for healing,
As if healing were "heaven enough"

> When we held each other up, dancing
> With the fire up the next gold hill.
> The little kick I learned in lemon crocuses.
> We danced more human, or so we assumed,
>
> Because the old habits overvalued
> What comes in to fill the absences,
> The sleeping sunlight where the family passes on.
>
> The losses, the nectar there: Blood, taken up,
> Is passed to us with such serenity.
>
> "Serenity!" But it was because we broke him
> Between us like bread. Because
"More human" was a healing-being-woundedness,
Not human enough, not a gladness fleshed.

The faun gazing on wine leaps away from us.
We were running now for the last hill,
The rumpled gold mess we called a bed.

And will I raise the wet walls whitewashed over us,
And the long red beams?

Will he keep the door open
As the flowers open which is not long?
This will be the wonder of experience:
What we found was more than we were left on the hill.

IN THE FUTURE, CHEER

Will be the few apes
Released from heaven, landing
One after another, all summer long,
On the new green porch.

Bring the wheat pillows,
Millions of them; all the wine.
Sign indecent jokes: "Another chance."
Reading of it now

Is our reward, the better
Memory, the unregretted one.
Approach the page. I was awake a
Million years reading.

Nowhere else as calm.
It is hilarious.
We will lie in the dying grass.
Consider the cheer.

notes

The Feather President
In a Victorian Gothic spirit, IN GOD WE TRUST was added to U.S. currency during the Civil War. During the cold war, "under God" was added to the pledge of allegiance. "Blue Cross" is a health insurance provider.

Variations on a National Air
Lines 3 to 6 are from one of Mark Twain's editorials on the impeachment of President Andrew Johnson in 1868.

"Precious Things"
Line 5 is excerpted from Sir Thomas Wyatt's poem of that title. Lines 11 to 12 are from the anonymous poem "Precious Things" (*3000 Years of Black Poetry*, edited by Alan Lomax and Raoul Abdul, 1971).

Worship of Mars
Lines 67 to 71 make use of Adolf Hitler's correspondence.

Days of 1948
Paul Robeson (1898–1976) was a charismatic singer and political activist. He was also the first African American to play Othello in the United States. When Henry Wallace, one of FDR's vice presidents, ran for president as a Progressive against Truman, Robeson was mentioned as a running mate. In 1948 he testified before the Senate Judiciary Committee during hearings on the Mundt-Nixon bill; it required Communist and "Communist-front" organizations to register with the federal government. Former vice president Wallace considered the bill an effort "to frighten all American people into conformity and silence." Lines 50 to 51 quote then-Republican Senator Moore from Oklahoma. The poem is indebted to Milada Marsalka's letters to Elizabeth Lord Hall.

The *Et Tu* Etudes
Lines 18 to 19 are from Julius Caesar's *Gallic Wars*.

White Bottom Blues
Lines 13 to 15 refer to "Ma Rainey's Black Bottom Blues." "The Star-Spangled Banner," while written in 1814, became the national anthem in 1931. Prior to that time, the song was considered too militaristic and difficult to sing.

Complaint of the Poet to Her Purse
Line 15 quotes Chaucer's "Complaint of the Poet to His Purse."

"No Stamping or Whistling Allowed in This Comique!"
Lines 63 and 64 are from Milt Gross's *Dunt Esk!* (1927). Lines 102 and 105 use Mae West material.

acknowledgments

American Letters & Commentary: "Balm."

LIT: "Fold Here: For United States: Found Poems."

Literary Imagination: "Poem for the Wheat Penny (1909–1958)" is reprinted from vol. 4, no. 2, of *Literary Imagination: The Review of the Association of Literary Scholars and Critics* (copyright © 2002). Used by permission of The Association of Literary Scholars and Critics.

The New Republic: "The Festival Cheer" as "Romp."

The Paris Review: "Upon the Bed-Trick Played on Jack."

Partisan Review: "The Cheer Regained" reprinted from vol. LXVII, no. 2, 2001.

Prairie Schooner: "Crazy Horse in Wannsee," "Days of 1948," and "The Princess" reprinted by permission of the University of Nebraska Press (copyright © 2000 by the University of Nebraska Press).

Tin House: "I Saw in Late November Pumpkins," "White Bottom Blues."

Verse: "Worship of Mars," "'Worship of Venus.'"

The Yale Review: "Souvenir of the New World."

My Business Is Circumference: Poets on Influence and Mastery: "Complaint of the Poet to Her Purse" (Paul Dry Books, 2001).

Grateful acknowledgment is made to the National Endowment for the Arts for an individual fellowship awarded during the composition of this book.

The author also wishes to thank Susan Hahn, Mark Strand, Susan Wheeler, Stephen Yenser, and Alec Bernstein for critical support.

JUDITH HALL is the author of
To Put the Mouth To, which was
selected for the National Poetry
Series, and *Anatomy, Errata,* winner
of the Ohio State University
Press / *The Journal* Award in Poetry.
She has received grants from the
National Endowment for the Arts
and the Ingram Merrill Foundation.
Her poems have appeared in
numerous magazines. She serves as
the poetry editor of *The Antioch
Review* and teaches at the California
Institute of Technology.